The Wildlife Detectives

How Forensic Scientists Fight Crimes Against Nature

Donna M. Jackson

Photographs by Wendy Shattil *and* Bob Rozinski

T0089200

Houghton Mifflin Harcourt

Boston   New York

With much love to Mom and Dad —D.M.J.

To all the young people who learn to protect these glorious creatures —W.S. & B.R.

For information about permission to reproduce selections from this book, write to trade.permissions@hmhco.com
or to Permissions, Houghton Mifflin Harcourt Publishing Company, 3 Park Avenue, 19th Floor, New York, New York 10016.

www.hmhco.com

The Library of Congress has cataloged the hardcover edition as follows:
Jackson, Donna, 1959–
The wildlife detectives: how forensic scientists fight crimes against nature / by Donna M. Jackson ; photographs by Wendy Shattil and Bob Rozinski. p. cm.
Summary: Describes how the wildlife detectives at the National Fish and Wildlife Forensics Laboratory in Ashland, Oregon, analyze clues to catch and convict people responsible for crimes against animals.
1. Undercover wildlife agents—United States—Juvenile literature. 2. Game wardens—United States—Juvenile literature. 3. Poaching—United States—Prevention—Juvenile literature.
4. Wild animal trade—United States—Juvenile literature. 5. Wildlife conservation—United States—Juvenile literature. 6. Endangered species—United States—Juvenile literature.
[1. United States Fish & Wildlife Forensics Laboratory. 2. Detectives. 3. Poaching. 4. Wild animal trade. 5. Wildlife conservation. 6. Endangered species.] I. Shattil, Wendy, ill. II.
Rozinski, Robert, ill. III. Title.
HV7959.J33   2000   363.28—dc21   99-34857 CIP
Design by Mike Rapp, Gear/Nashville

ISBN: 978-0-395-86976-5 hardcover
ISBN: 978-0-618-19683-8 paperback

Manufactured in China
SCP 20 19 18 17 16

4500832153

Acknowledgments

Thanks to all who shared their time and talent in the making of this book, especially the dedicated scientists at the National Wildlife Forensics Lab: Ken Goddard, Ed Espinoza, Mary-Jacque Mann, Bonnie Yates, Peter Dratch, Jerry Ruth, Richard Stroud, Verlin Cross, Steven Fain, and Beth Ann Sabo; Pat Ozment; Special Agent Roy Brown; visionary Tom Grosz; Craig Hoover at TRAFFIC, North America; Vince Mautino; Norman "Joe" Schafer; Andy Long; Bob Christensen; Assistant U.S. Attorney Kip Crofts; Mary Tabor; Jones Benally and his family; Sergeant Mark Olin and Detectives Ed Frushour, Frank Kerber, and Pat Quinlan; Bill Adrian, Patt Dorsey, David Croonquist at the Colorado Division of Wildlife; Bernadette Hilbourn; Cindy Reinitz; and Ryan Fisher.

Special thanks to Wendy Shattil and Bob Rozinski for their exquisite wildlife photographs; to Stu Mitchell and Darby Morrell for helping us fill in the gaps with Wildlife Laboratory photos; to Paul Malinowski, for having a sense of humor; to Ann Rider, for her encouragement, support, and patience; to Megan Tingley, for her gracious redirections; and to the loves of my life, Charlie and Christopher Jackson, for riding the roller coaster with me! —D.M.J.

Our thanks go to Donna Jackson, who imagined a book on a matter dear to our hearts. We're grateful for the opportunity to use our photos to protect wildlife and educate young people. Our visit to the U.S. Fish and Wildlife Forensics Lab introduced us to exceptionally skilled scientists who are dedicated to defending injustices against animals helpless to speak for themselves. —W.S. & B.R.

CONTENTS

THE WILDLIFE DETECTIVES

Sea turtles face extinction because people hunt them for food.

It was the last straw.

Eleven thousand pounds of meat from illegally killed green sea turtles were sitting at a New York airport, and Terry Grosz could do nothing about it.

Eleven thousand pounds. That meant more than one hundred endangered sea turtles had been slaughtered to make soup.

"What should we do?" the airport's wildlife inspectors asked Grosz, a law enforcement officer at the U.S. Fish and Wildlife Service's Endangered

Endangered Species desk in Washington, D.C. The inspectors *knew* the meat belonged to the rare green sea turtle, which was illegal to kill. But how could they prove it beyond a doubt so that they could arrest the people responsible?

Grosz sprang into action. "I frantically called all over the country trying to get someone to identify the sea turtle meat," he says. "But no one could help me—the DNA expertise [on animals] was just nonexistent."

Soon the meat merchants protested. Seize the meat or let the shipment go through before it spoils, they insisted. If not, we'll sue.

Unable to find anyone who could help, Grosz reluctantly released the turtle meat for sale and watched the suspects walk away. This wasn't the first time Grosz had seen a crime against wildlife go unpunished for lack of scientific evidence. But he wanted it to be the last.

"What we need is a forensics lab dedicated to solving wildlife crimes," he told the chief of the Law Enforcement Division at the U.S. Fish and Wildlife Service. Twelve years later, Grosz realized his dream.

Today, thoughtless people continue to steal shamelessly from nature. They gun down bears for their gallbladders, shoot eagles for their feathers, and slaughter elephants for their ivory. Unfortunately, as many as 90 percent of these criminals go unpunished because there aren't enough wildlife agents, inspectors, and other resources to stop them.

But the tide is turning. These days, whenever officers recover evidence from a wildlife crime scene, finding scientific clues to catch and convict the criminals is significantly easier. That's because the Wildlife Detectives at the National Fish and Wildlife Forensics Laboratory in Ashland, Oregon, work behind the microscopes.

The Wildlife Detectives hunt down and analyze every kind of clue, from DNA, bone fragments, and bloodstains to firearms, fibers, and footprints. Just as police detectives in crime labs sift through evidence to solve human crimes, the Wildlife Detectives apply their expert skills to fight crimes against animals.

The U.S. Fish and Wildlife Forensics Laboratory in Ashland, Oregon, is the first of its kind in the world.

Before the lab opened in 1989, most wildlife crime cases were difficult to prove in court. The animals weren't talking, and neither were the suspects. "You practically had to catch someone in the act to convict them," says Ken Goddard, director of the laboratory.

Now wildlife agencies from around the world call on the Wildlife Detectives to help them crack difficult cases. One famous case that the Wildlife Detectives investigated began in the alpine meadows of Yellowstone National Park.

Precious and Few

Before human beings arrived, only one out of a million species died of natural causes every year. . . . (Today) we are killing tens of thousands of species every year.
—"The Endangered 100," *Life*, September 1994

What is an endangered species?

Any species considered to be in immediate danger of extinction. Tigers are endangered, with only 5,000 to 7,000 left prowling the earth—a 95 percent reduction since 1900.

What is a threatened species?

Any species likely to become endangered within the foreseeable future. The Mexican spotted owl, the gray wolf, and the grizzly bear are all threatened species. While some species are making a comeback, they are still considered to be at risk.

How do humans contribute to the death of species?

• **Poaching** Illegally killing or capturing wildlife. For example, black rhino populations are plummeting partly because the animals are killed for their horns.

• **Destroying natural habitats** As human populations grow and nations become industrialized, we use more land to build homes, offices, and shopping centers. We also use the earth's natural resources, such as oil, wood, and coal. This shrinks wildlands and destroys the homes of many species.

• **Introducing exotic species** Bringing new species into an area often threatens the native animals. Foxes released by fur traders in the Aleutian Islands of Alaska several decades ago nearly destroyed the Aleutian Canada goose.

• **Polluting the environment** Poisons on land, in the oceans and lakes, and in the air can cause long-lasting damage to people and animals.

Clockwise from the top: red wolf; Mexican spotted owl; grizzly bear with twins; black rhinos

MYSTERY IN THE MEADOWS

September 18, 1993

An eerie sound echoes through the crisp evening air at Yellowstone National Park. It is mating season, and the bull elk are bugling to attract cows (female elk) and fend off other males. In a meadow known as Elk Park, a brawny bull elk nicknamed Charger stands at attention, steam rising from his mouth. He hears the trumpeting of a rival, a strapping young bull aiming to steal his cows.

Charger's burly body stiffens as he tilts back his mighty antlers and stretches his thick neck. He lets loose a warning bugle call that begins with an ominous deep whistle and rises to a hauntingly high pitch. The intruder gets

Majestic animals, such as Charger, attract photographers.

the message.

Click. Flash. Click, click. Flash. Click, click, click . . .

A long line of visitors and wildlife photographers capture the moment with their cameras. This is nothing new for Charger; he is one of Yellowstone's star attractions, with his grand physique and magnificent set of antlers.

One admirer is Vince Mautino, a photographer from Colorado. "This particular night, there were probably two hundred people crowded around watching him," Vince says. "He was only ten or fifteen yards off the road, and he'd go up in the timber and come back and run his cows around."

Vince and his wife photographed Charger until dusk that Saturday night. They planned to return early Sunday morning for more.

September 19, 1993

Silence hangs over Elk Park.

"We came back, and there were no elk present at all," Vince says. "It was really weird, because this meadow always has elk in it, and to have them completely disappear was really strange."

One of the largest bull elk in Yellowstone, who weighed about 800 pounds, Charger survived the fires in 1988 that destroyed a fifth of the park. This photo was taken the day before Charger was killed.

Vince and his wife stopped to photograph some geese and then moved on to a nearby meadow. Still no elk.

"So we went back down near the Gibbon River at Elk Park and looked out about one hundred and fifty yards into the meadow. That's when we saw this brown lump. It looked like an elk lying there, but there sure wasn't one lying there last night," he says.

Vince and several other photographers hiked to the site and discovered the body of a big bull elk lying on the grass near the water.

Vince knew immediately. The slain elk was Charger.

11

Animal Crime Lab

Mounted birds perched on file cabinets. Cougar skins draped across stainless steel tables. A liquid-nitrogen freezer housing thousands of animal blood and tissue samples.

It's not your typical crime laboratory. Then again, the Wildlife Forensics Lab in Ashland, Oregon, is the only full-service animal crime lab in the world. Each day the receiving room of the Evidence and Property Section overflows with new arrivals.

"Once we were told a whale was coming," says director Ken Goddard. "We didn't know if that meant the whole animal or just a part. Fortunately, it was just a part."

After the evidence is checked in, it is sent to the different departments of the lab. "All crime labs basically do the same thing," explains Goddard, who once worked as a police detective in California. "First we identify evidence. In our case, we match animal pieces, parts, or products back to the species."

Once the animal species is known, the lab works to link the suspect, the victim, and the crime scene. It's nearly impossible for

these three elements to come together without leaving a trace. "That's what we're doing when we match bullets in an animal carcass back to a suspect's weapon or compare a gut pile on the ground to meat in someone's freezer or to a head on the wall," Goddard says.

Answering these questions for the more than one million animal species protected by law worldwide presents quite a challenge. That's why it takes a highly skilled team of forensic scientists working together to solve wildlife crimes.

In the **Morphology Section,** experts on reptiles, amphibians, birds, and mammals identify evidence by examining such parts as bones, fur, and claws. To help with identification, the scientists have amassed a "comparison" collection of specimens, including wolf skulls and rhino heads.

Serologists analyze blood and body fluids to match the blood on a weapon to a victim, to determine an animal's species and sex, and to decide whether two or more specimens came from the same animal. In some cases, they can even determine the identity of a victim's parents.

In **Criminalistics,** firearms experts and chemists use a $250,000 scanning electron microscope and other high-tech tools to analyze everything from soil and tire tracks to elephant ivory and exotic medicines containing wildlife ingredients. They can also match bullets to guns and paint chips to crime scenes.

Pathologists perform necropsies—autopsies for animals—to establish the cause of death. "It's important that we don't confuse an animal killing another for food or terri-tory with a human violation of laws," says Goddard.

What's the most difficult part of the job? Figuring out new ways to identify species from just their parts, says Goddard. "If people sent whole animals to be identified, we wouldn't need a lab," he explains.

Clockwise from top right: Richard Stroud comparing X-ray with bird specimen; Beth Ann Sabo examining bird skins and feathers; Steven Fain taking samples

13

HUNTING CLUES

Photographer Vince Mautino telephones Yellowstone Park officials. Soon rangers arrive at Elk Park, where Charger lies dead.

"We thought the elk had been hit by a car," says Ranger Mary Tabor. "Then we saw the bullet holes."

Park rangers secure the area and begin investigating. First they examine the elk. "The animal was lying on its left side with its head to the north," Tabor describes in her report. "The antlers and skullcap had been removed. All the other body parts were intact . . . There was a large puddle of blood on the ground behind the animal's withers and a small puddle below the head wound."

Closer observation reveals that Charger has been shot at least three times—twice in the body and once in the head. Rangers remove two bullets from the animal's body and

Park rangers examine Charger and collect evidence at the crime scene.

send them to the Wyoming State Crime Lab in Cheyenne to be identified.

After examining Charger, rangers collect other crime-scene clues. These include a crushed .25-caliber (diameter) shell casing that appears to have been run over by a car or a truck and a box of .25-caliber rifle ammunition found on the side of the road about one mile south of the crime scene. The box contains seven cartridges and four used shell casings.

Based on this evidence, investigators surmise that the weapon used was a .25-caliber rifle —an unusual caliber.

Next, rangers interview park visitors for eyewitness accounts of the incident. They ask questions such as "When was the last time you saw the animal?" "Was anyone unusual in the area?" "Did you hear any gunshots?"

Campers at Norris Campground, about a mile and a half away from the crime scene, say they heard at least one shot at about 8:30 P.M. on Saturday night but did not report it.

One man says he saw a "suspicious" white pickup truck in Elk Park at about 10:30 P.M. that night. When passengers in the truck spotted him, they sped from the area, drove for about a mile and a half, and turned into the Gibbon River picnic area. The man saw the truck's brake lights flash, but when he followed the truck to the picnic area, it sped away to the north.

Could the people in the truck have been involved with Charger's death? Park rangers and the U.S. Fish and Wildlife Service intend to find out.

It's the Law

Early American settlers commonly hunted wild animals, for game was plentiful, and killing for food was considered a right. As time passed and cities grew, however, wildlife populations became threatened by "market" hunters, who killed animals to satisfy people's demands for fancy feathered hats and elegant wildlife cuisine.

In 1872 Congress limited market hunting and established Yellowstone National Park for the benefit of people and wildlife. But illegal kills continued in the park, and in 1886 the army stepped in to restore order and enforce the laws.

By the turn of the century, market hunters had taken such a large toll on species nationwide that Congress passed the first major U.S. legislation to protect wildlife. The Lacey Act of 1900 prohibited the interstate transport of any wildlife or wildlife product taken in violation of state law, paving the way for future laws protecting wildlife. These include:

• **The Migratory Bird Treaty Act of 1916,** between Canada and the United States, makes it unlawful to hunt, kill, capture, keep, buy, sell, or trade any migratory bird or its feathers, nests, and eggs.

• **The Bald Eagle Protection Act of 1940** makes it illegal to import, export, hunt, harm, or harass bald or golden eagles. People also cannot sell, buy, or trade bald eagle parts, nests, eggs, or products. The only exception involves the use by Native Americans of eagle feathers for religious ceremonies.

• **The Marine Mammal Protection Act of 1972** bans the possession of marine mammals, such as otters and walruses, and their importation into the United States. A special exception is made for Alaska natives who hunt marine mammals for food or make handicrafts to support themselves.

• **The Endangered Species Act of 1973** makes it illegal to import, export, take, possess, harm, sell, or transport any threatened or endangered species across state and national boundaries. The law was developed in response to wildlife trade that was rapidly depleting animals throughout the world.

• **CITES,** the Convention on International Trade in Endangered Species of Wild Fauna and Flora, goes hand in hand with the Endangered Species Act. Under this agreement, more than 120 nations have regulated international wildlife trade to help prevent the extinction of threatened or potentially threatened species.

• **The African Elephant Conservation Act of 1989** prohibits the importation of any African elephant ivory or African elephant item into the United States for commercial purposes because the species is threatened. Exporting ivory also is prohibited. (The act does not apply to ivory brought into the country before 1989.)

One of only two species of eagles in the United States, the bald eagle is protected under federal law.

REWARD FOR INFORMATION

September 1993

After media reports of Charger's death, the National Park Service receives hundreds of letters and telephone calls from citizens and organizations nationwide. Many donate money to a reward fund for the capture and conviction of the poachers.

Meanwhile, the U.S. Fish and Wildlife Service teams with the National Park Service and other government agencies to solve the puzzle of the

Bullets come in a variety of shapes and sizes. One way firearms experts match bullets to a crime scene is to examine details such as the caliber of the bullet and microscopic impressions left by the barrel of the gun.

beloved elk's death.

"We really wanted to catch this person because of the brazenness of going into the crown jewel of the national parks and killing a well-known animal," Special Agent Jim Klett tells reporters. Klett, who coordinated the overall investigation for the U.S. Fish and Wildlife Service, pulled together evidence from other wildlife agents, such as Pat Ozment, who was in charge of the case at Yellowstone.

"At this point, we had already collected some good leads," Ozment says. "We had several suspect vehicles, and a lot of people came forward to help." One woman even agreed to be hypnotized so she could recall a license plate number, although that effort failed.

Firearms experts at the Wyoming State Crime Lab confirm that the bullets removed from Charger are indeed the same unusual caliber as those found at the crime scene.

"We think that after the poachers killed the elk, they probably stood out by the side of the truck and put the box of shells on the fender or bumper," says Ozment. "When they heard someone coming, they probably were scared, and the box fell off as the vehicle fled."

Now the goal was to locate the rifle and/or the missing antlers so that investigators could scientifically link the evidence to the killer.

Ozment alerted the FBI to calls he had received about elk racks (antlers) being shipped out of Salt Lake City, Utah, and distributed a press release with sketches of Charger's antlers to sheriffs' departments.

The National Park Service also ran an article with a photo about Charger in the Rocky Mountain Elk Foundation's fall issue of *Bugle* magazine: "The National Park Service and the U.S. Fish and Wildlife Service are offering a reward for information leading to the arrest and conviction of the poachers. If you have any information regarding this incident or the whereabouts of the antlers, please call . . ."

In Utah, taxidermist Norman "Joe" Schafer reads the *Bugle* article with interest. The antlers look familiar. Didn't someone bring in an elk rack like this a few weeks before to be mounted?

Wild File

Poaching for Profit

The illegal traffic in wild animals and their parts and products is estimated to be worth as much as $5 billion a year. Whale teeth sell for $2,000 apiece. A tiger skin may bring in up to $10,000, and an elk head with an impressive set of antlers may be marketed for $20,000.

In January 1999, state and federal officers arrested almost three dozen people in Virginia and charged them with crimes related to killing bears for their gallbladders. Bear galls are often an ingredient in traditional Asian medicines and are used to cure all types of ailments, from backaches to heart disease.

"Since the substantial decline of the Asian bear populations, the American black bear has been targeted for this trade," says a Virginia Department of Game official. "One bear gallbladder may sell overseas at auction for thousands of dollars. Dried and ground to a fine powder, it is sold by the gram at a street value greater than that of cocaine."

Poachers break wildlife laws by:
• Killing endangered or threatened species
• Smuggling and/or peddling wild animals and parts
• Using spotlights at night to stun, trap, and turn animals into easy targets
• Hunting out of season, or in areas where it is prohibited, such as national parks
• Exceeding hunting license limits

Some people poach to put food on the table, to bag a trophy for the mantel, or to experience a thrill. Others poach for profit— buying and selling illegal wildlife for big money. They are commercial poachers.

Among the animals most threatened by commercial poachers are tigers, rhinos, and sea turtles, says Craig Hoover, program officer for TRAFFIC,* North America, a wildlife trade and monitoring program of the World Wildlife Fund (an organization that works to save wildlife and its habitats).

"Sea turtles are preyed upon throughout their life history," Hoover says. Their nests are raided for eggs so people can eat them, their leather is used to make boots, and their shells are cleaned and shellacked for display.

Just about every part of the tiger is in demand for use in traditional Asian medicines. The brains are used to help treat pimples, the whiskers to alleviate toothaches, and the tail to remedy skin diseases.

Live animals, such as parrots and reptiles, are also illegally traded. Each year, thousands of macaws, lizards, boa constrictors, and other "exotic" animals are stolen from the wild and smuggled across borders to be sold as pets.

How do importers smuggle these creatures across national borders?

"You name it, it's been tried," says Hoover. "I've seen animals smuggled in suitcases, stuffed into shoes and socks, and hidden in spare tires."

One man smuggled a live toucan into the country by taping it to the small of this back, and a woman tried to conceal a spider monkey in her hair.

Many of these illegally transported animals die before reaching their destination. Still, the few that do make it to the marketplace bring such high profits, that the importers can "afford" the loss.

In the United States, where the demand for wildlife and wildlife products is greater than anywhere else in the world, programs have been set up to educate consumers who may unknowingly purchase illegal pets or animal products, such as alligator-skin handbags. Antipoaching programs also encourage citizens to anonymously report suspicious activities in their states. These programs offer rewards for information leading to the arrest of wildlife criminals.

* TRAFFIC stands for Trade Records Analysis of Flora and Fauna in Commerce.

Clockwise from the top right: American alligator; scarlet macaw; bear gallbladder products; feather headdress; tiger wading in shallow water

THE TINES THAT BIND

November 12, 1993

The phone rings at Pat Ozment's office in Yellowstone.

It is the taxidermist from Utah, Joe Schafer. He has read the *Bugle* article and thinks that the elk rack left in his shop for mounting might belong to Charger.

Ozment asks him, "Who brought the antlers in? When did you receive them? Was anyone else with the suspect?"

Schafer carefully answers each question.

Elk shed their antlers each winter. But that doesn't stop people from killing elk to get antlers.

"Someone from the Fish and Wildlife Service will call you within a half-hour," Ozment says. Meanwhile, using the FBI's computer databases, he runs a license check on the person named by Schafer: Jack Porter,* a blond man with blue eyes in his early twenties.

Jim Klett telephones the taxidermist to say he is sending an agent to look at the rack.

A few days later, Special Agent Roy Brown, from Salt Lake City, arrives at Schafer's motor-boat repair and taxidermy shop. Brown snakes his way through the boats sitting in the shop and introduces himself to Schafer, who is fixing an engine. He shows Schafer his badge, which identifies him as a federal law enforcement officer, and the men talk for an hour.

Schafer tells Brown that sometime around October 22, Jack Porter came into his shop. "He carried in a large, six-by-eight-point, nontypical bull elk rack and asked if I would mount it for him. I asked him where he got such a nice bull. He said that he had shot the animal up in the Salmon, Idaho, area."

Brown examines the antlers. Their unique shape and a missing tine indicate that they probably came from Charger. But only the Wildlife Detectives would be able to tell for certain, so he seizes the antlers as evidence.

23

After leaving the shop, Brown uncovers some more information. He learns that Porter owns a four-wheel-drive white Ford pickup with a ladder rack and that he manages his own general contracting business. When Brown searches the FBI's National Crime Information Center files, he discovers that Porter has no criminal record. He then reviews the databases at the state fish and game agencies and finds that Porter holds licenses to hunt deer in Utah and to hunt elk in Idaho.

Once the background check is completed, Brown contacts Pat Ozment back at Yellowstone. It is time to pay a visit to the suspect.

*To respect the privacy of his family, the suspect's name has been changed. All other names, dates, and circumstances are real.

Heartbreak Zoo

Snakeskin sneakers. Polar bear rugs. Caiman-foot keychains. Walk the aisles of the National Wildlife Property Repository near Denver, Colorado, and these are some of the heartbreaking exhibits you'll see lining the shelves.

One aisle contains python, crocodile, and other reptile skins that have been fashioned into fancy belts, handbags, and cowboy boots. Another holds exotic medicines prepared with bear gallbladders, deer antlers, tiger bones, and other wildlife ingredients. Nearby are the cat aisle, the sea turtle aisle, and the North American mammal aisle, each displaying a wide range of wildlife objects. In all, more than 300,000 illegally killed animals and products created with them dwell in this gloomy one-of-a-kind zoo.

"We're the only place in the country that receives wildlife items that have been forfeited or abandoned to the U.S. Fish and Wildlife Service," explains Bernadette Hilbourn, a specialist at the repository. "All wildlife that's confiscated as a result of any kind of wildlife violation, whether it's an import or an export, generally comes here,"* she says. "Once a case goes to court and closes, the evidence becomes government property and is sent to us to store."

What does the repository do with these sad souvenirs?

Wildlife agents use some of the items to catch poachers. They donate others to museums for science exhibits and to schools for wildlife education. Items that are in really bad shape are incinerated.

The most tragic aspect of this collection, however, is that the repository holds just a small percentage of the wildlife that has been killed illegally—all in the name of fashion, greed, vanity, and superstition.

*When officers confiscate live animals, they usually donate them to zoos because in many cases the animals cannot readapt to the wild. Also, they may carry infectious diseases picked up during their capture.

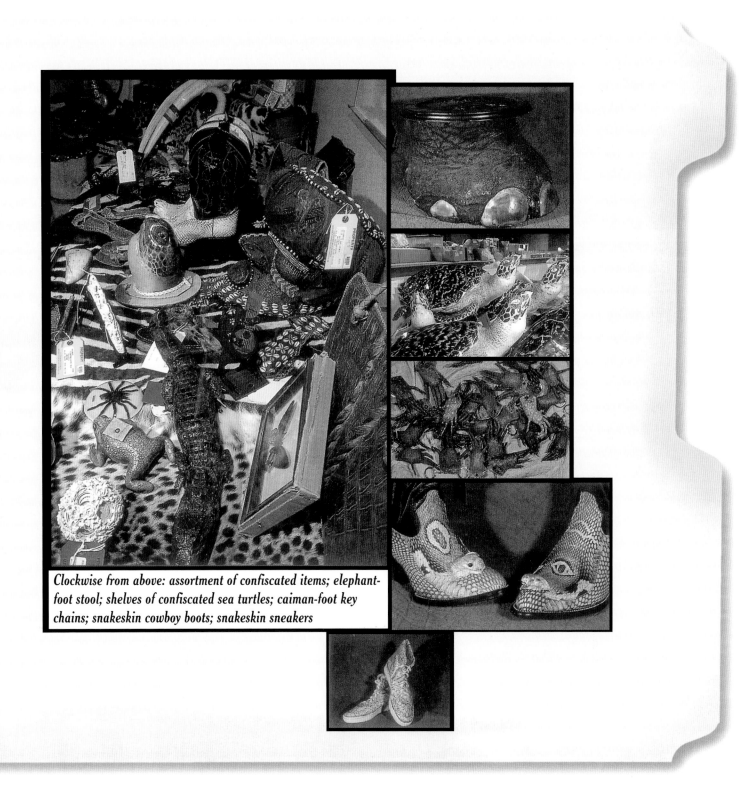

Clockwise from above: assortment of confiscated items; elephant-foot stool; shelves of confiscated sea turtles; caiman-foot key chains; snakeskin cowboy boots; snakeskin sneakers

ANTLERS AND ALIBIS

December 2, 1993

Investigator Pat Ozment from Yellowstone joins Agent Roy Brown in Salt Lake City to meet with the suspect, Jack Porter.

Where were you when the elk was killed? Brown asks Porter. And how did you come upon these antlers?

Porter says that on September 18, he and an employee went to Idaho to repair a roof. While he was working there, he needed some supplies and

Bighorn sheep horns bring $8,000 to $10,000.

Black rhino horns may yield $10,000 and up.

called a friend. Later that evening the friend returned his call and invited him to go elk hunting.

"That night I met [my friend] at the Sinclair gas station . . . and we dropped my truck off at his house," says Porter's official statement. Then they drove to the mountains. "Early on the morning of the 20th, we [rode] the horses up to the area we hunted. We called in some elk and [my friend] shot the third bull that we called in."

They then went back to his friend's house, Porter says, and his friend offered him the elk rack in exchange for his help.

Tell me more about your friend, Brown says. But Porter cannot remember the man's address and phone number.

Next, the agents ask about Porter's guns. What type did he use, and did he have any of his guns with him?

As it turns out, he had quite a few fancy guns, including one similar to the rifle used to shoot Charger. Brown says, "So we got talking about it, and he said, 'Oh, that one's up in Idaho, it's not here right now.'"

Brown asks Porter to bring the rifle in so that the crime lab can establish whether the bullets that killed Charger were shot from his gun. Porter agrees, saying that the next time he goes to his parents' house in Idaho, he will bring back the gun.

Although the suspected rifle is not available to inspect, bullets are. With some clever talking, the agents persuade Porter to give them two boxes of .25-caliber rounds, including some shell casings that had already been shot through his rifle.

After the interview, Ozment submits the cartridges and casings to the Wyoming State Crime Lab to compare to those recovered at the crime scene.

Will they match? The investigators will know soon.

December 8, 1993

Porter telephones Agent Brown, saying he has the rifle he used in Idaho. Should he drop it by?

"Sure, come right over," says Brown.

Porter and one of his employees arrive at the U.S. Fish and Wildlife Service Law Enforcement office in Salt Lake City. He hands Brown a Ruger M-77, .25-caliber bolt-action rifle.

"It's a shame people go into national parks and kill nice critters that belong to all of us," Brown says to the two men. "You'd think someone with a real conscience who knew about this wouldn't put up with it."

A few weeks later, Brown receives a mysterious phone call.

"I need to talk to you," says the voice on the other end of the line. "I know who killed the elk in Yellowstone."

28

An elk head may sell for as much as $20,000.

Operation Ivory

Poachers love ivory, and it's easy to understand why. One large elephant tusk can sell for as much as $7,000. After that it can be carved into exquisite jewelry and other fine pieces of art to generate even more money.

But poaching ivory has another price—the lives of African and Asian elephants. According to the World Wildlife Fund, only about 30,000 to 40,000 Asian elephants remain in the wild, and the population of African elephants has dropped from about 1.2 million in the late 1970s to about 600,000 today.

In 1989, to help stop the rapid decline of the African elephant, the United States made it illegal to import the endangered animal's ivory into this country. However, it was still legal to import ivory from mammoth tusks and other ivorylike materials. This made it difficult for wildlife inspectors to tell the difference between legal and illegal ivory. Many people claimed that their ivory tusks came from mammoths, whether or not they really did. Mammoths, relatives of today's elephant, have been extinct for about 10,000 years. Still, at least 13 million pounds of their ancient ivory exists worldwide, preserved in the Arctic as buried fossils. Importing this ivory is legal because it does not harm an existing species.

Recognizing the ivory identification problem, officials called the Wildlife Forensics Lab for help.

Five months later, scientists Ed Espinoza and Mary-Jacque Mann developed a technique that distinguished between elephant ivory and other forms of ivory, using a $250,000 scanning electron microscope and a 25-cent protractor. After reading everything they could about ivory and taking thousands of measurements, the pair discovered that the patterns of tiny lines (called Schreger lines) in elephant ivory form different angles from the lines in mammoth ivory. Mann explains:

- If the Schreger angles in an ivory object average 115 degrees or more, then the object is made of elephant ivory.
- If the Schreger angles average 90 degrees or less, the object is made of mammoth ivory.

When an object doesn't fall into either category, there are still ways to tell whether the material comes from the tusk of a walrus, narwhal, or warthog or the tooth of a killer whale or hippopotamus.

With the discovery of Schreger lines, the lab not only solved a problem that had baffled scientists for more than one hundred years, it found an identification technique that proved to be an enormous deterrent to criminals, explains Espinoza.

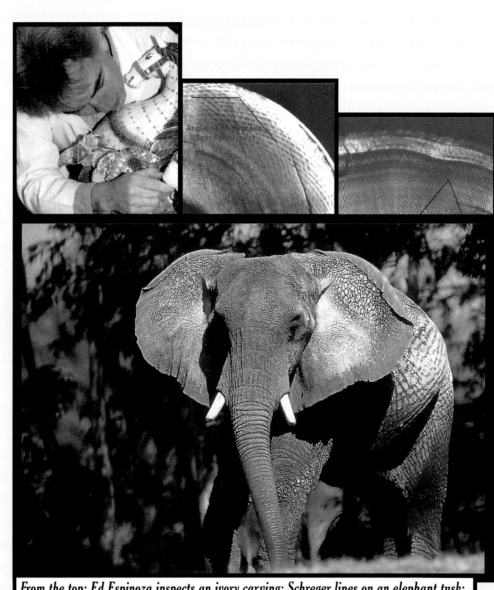

From the top: Ed Espinoza inspects an ivory carving; Schreger lines on an elephant tusk; Schreger lines on a mammoth tusk; an endangered African elephant

UNDER THE MICROSCOPE

Dr. Jerry Ruth analyzes DNA to identify wildlife victims such as Charger.

January/February 1994

A series of packages arrives at the U.S. Fish and Wildlife Service Forensics Lab in Ashland. One box contains the frozen head of a bull elk; the second, a pair of antlers attached to a skull plate. The third holds eleven 35-mm slides and three photo negatives of a bull elk.

All involve Case No. 1197AP—the slaying of Charger the bull elk.

According to the background information included with the evidence, the elk had been shot and killed in Yellowstone National Park. Wildlife officials there want the lab to:

- Decide whether the elk antlers and the elk head are from the same animal.
- Compare the antlers with those on the elk in the slides and negatives to determine if they are the same.
- Compare the skull plate attached to the antlers with the frozen elk skull to see if the saw (or tool) marks and other cuts match.

After Evidence and Property officers log the items into the lab's computer system and label them with green evidence tags, they forward the specimens to Dr. Jerry Ruth, who leads the investigation at the lab.

On February 9, Dr. Ruth sends tissue samples to Dr. Peter Dratch, a forensic serologist at the lab, who analyzes blood and body fluids.

"My job was to verify the species," says Dr. Dratch.

To do this, Dr. Dratch begins by establishing the animal's scientific family. Using immunodiffusion, a lab test that compares antibodies, he finds that the specimens contain tissue from a member of the deer family, Cervidae.

Verlin Cross examines photographic evidence for wildlife cases.

"Now there are about forty species of deer worldwide, but only five in North America," says Dr. Dratch. "Those are white-tailed deer, mule deer, elk, moose, and caribou. So once I know this is a deer, and it's a case from the United States, I'm going to primarily focus on those five species."

Further testing reveals that the samples match tissue from elk (*Cervus elaphus*) and no other species in the North American deer family.

Once Dr. Dratch verifies that the samples are elk, Dr. Ruth develops DNA (deoxyribonucleic acid) profiles of each specimen to determine whether they come from the *same* animal.

Inside the cells of every animal—including humans—are chemicals containing secret codes identifying who or what we are. These DNA molecules, which determine every physical characteristic from eye color to body size, give scientists a genetic clue that they can use for identification.

Using DNA profiling, Dr. Ruth compares samples—one from the elk rack and one from the elk head—to see if they come from the same animal. (Coincidentally, the DNA test relies on an enzyme produced by bacteria discovered in hot springs at Yellowstone National Park, not far from where Charger lived.)

The DNA profiles or "fingerprints" match, indicating that the head and the rack almost certainly came from the same animal.

"The probability that two unrelated North American elk will have the same DNA profiles is estimated at one in more than one hundred thousand," says Dr. Ruth.

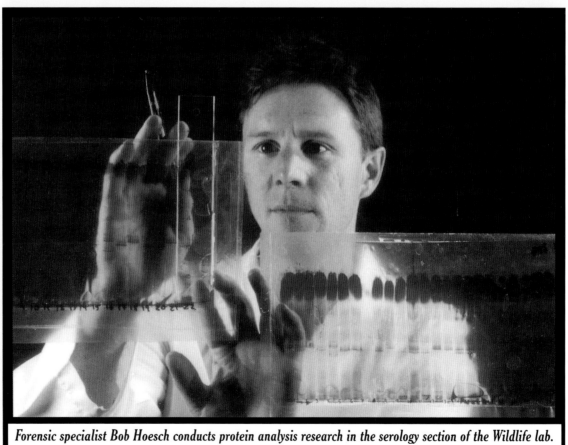

Forensic specialist Bob Hoesch conducts protein analysis research in the serology section of the Wildlife lab.

33

Eagle Express

Recycling birds. Sounds strange, but that's the job of the National Eagle Repository in Colorado. When bald or golden eagles and other raptors die from natural causes or at the hands of people, wildlife agents send them to the repository. Here the birds are stored and eventually distributed to Native Americans.

"Under the Bald Eagle Protection Act, Native Americans are authorized to use eagle feathers for religious ceremonial purposes," explains Bernadette Hilbourn. "So we ship whole carcasses, parts, or just feathers to American Indians throughout the country." Native Americans must have a permit from the government to obtain eagle feathers or parts.

Eagles are symbols of great strength, courage, and wisdom to Native Americans, who weave the feathers into ceremonial war bonnets, whistles, and jewelry. Many eagle feathers are used in Native American ceremonies, such as powwows. Wing feathers are made into plumes to decorate dancers' headdresses, while tail feathers transform into traditional fans.

Jones Benally, a Navajo medicine man from Arizona, recently applied for an eagle.

"Eagle feathers are very sacred to us," Benally says. "They're used in many religious ceremonies, including prayer services for those who are troubled and ceremonies for the dead."

When people become ill, Benally also uses eagle feathers as part of his healing ritual. "The feather I'm using now is more than a couple of hundred years old," he says. "It was passed down to me from my grandfather, who received it from his grandfather."

Navajo medicine man Jones Benally uses eagle feathers in rituals to help heal the sick.

The Eagle Repository replaces broken or unusable feathers before shipping them to Native Americans. Bottom: Bald eagles have wingspans of up to eight feet and may weigh as much as fifteen pounds.

THE MATCH GAME

Once the DNA profiles have been matched, Bonnie Yates in the forensic lab's Morphology Section examines the rest of the elk. Her assignment is to determine if the antlers and elk head belong to the elk pictured in one or more of the slides and to compare the saw marks on the edges of the skull plate with the marks on the top of the elk head to see if they match.

"The segment that was given to me specifically was a bag with a big frozen head in it and an enormous rack of antlers," says Yates, coordinator of the lab's mammals unit, who has a master's degree in archaeozoology. "The antlers were together on a skull plate that had been cut off the head," she says. And the head had a "big gaping hole in it. The question to me was, could I say with certainty that this rack came off this head?"

To find out, Yates first positions the two pieces together. They fit—but not exactly.

Bonnie Yates measures a bear claw with calipers.

"When you use a chain saw or any kind of saw to remove a rack from a head, there's invariably a gap that's exactly the width of the saw blade, so it will never fit back like a jigsaw puzzle or a broken piece of crockery," she says. The saw-blade portion disappears into bone dust.

Since it is impossible to demonstrate a precise fit, Yates uses modeling clay to take an impression of the saw (or tool)

Morphologists compare and contrast bones to solve wildlife crimes.

marks on the head and the skull plate to see if the patterns match. With tissue and hair stuck to the quarter-inch-thick rim of the skull, the task is a messy one.

"I got a hair dryer because I didn't want to let the whole head defrost," Yates explains. "I knew it would be a real stinky mess, so I took the dryer and defrosted the rim of the skull—just enough so I could brush off the matter with a toothbrush and get a clean impression."

Yates lifts impressions from the rim of the elk's head and then from the rim of the skull plate. The anatomy of the elk's skull allows her to cast pieces that are as much as an inch wide, giving her a clear look at the direction of the saw marks.

"That was really the key," she says. "Not the actual impression of the saw marks, but their direction."

Were the marks going in the same direction over the right eye of the animal? How about over the left ear? "I had to see that they were going in the same direction for the correct anatomical part of the skull," she says.

After carefully comparing marks, Yates determines that the head and the rack are a positive match.

Next, she compares the elk specimens with photos of Charger taken by park visitors. Yates enlarges several key photos that show various views of the elk's head and antlers. Then she positions the antlers to match some of the views in the pictures and photographs them for comparison.

"The rack wasn't too difficult to match because it belonged to a big bull elk, and the older bulls get, the more individuality their antlers have," Yates says. "This one had a lot of smaller points, including a ring of small tines, called a little royal."

Yates quickly makes a positive identification: the rack of antlers confiscated from the taxidermist's shop matches the antlers in the photographs.

Slain Charger

Birds of a Feather

Some people read palms to predict the future. Beth Ann Sabo reads feathers to peek at the past. Sabo is a forensic ornithologist—a scientist who studies birds and identifies their remains to help solve wildlife crimes.

What kinds of crimes do people commit against birds?

Some shoot ducks and other migratory birds for food or fun; some smuggle wild parrots into the United States to sell as pets; and some trap falcons and other birds of prey to be sold as hunting birds for as much as $100,000. In Idaho, one person shot eagles off power poles so he could sell their wings and feet as ornaments.

Sabo helps nab these criminals by identifying everything from whole birds to bird parts.

Once a poacher tried to erase all the evidence that might be used against him by burning the birds he had killed illegally. But Sabo still retrieved plenty of clues, "because he hadn't destroyed the bones, and some of the feathers on the underside had been protected." Those feathers supplied all the information Sabo needed to send the man's alibi up in smoke. Her conclusion? He had illegally killed six birds, including an owl, a falcon, and a rough-legged hawk.

"When making an identification, the goal is usually to recognize features of the bird that place it in an order, family, and possibly even a species," says Sabo, who apprenticed at the Smithsonian Institution for six years in feather and bird identification.

With nearly 8,700 species of birds worldwide and about 900 species in the United States, this can be a challenge. To complicate matters, within one species, birds may vary in appearance according to sex, age, season, or location. For example, ducks go through a molting phase, when they lose all their showy feathers. A bird shot during that phase looks very different from one of the same species shot during hunting season, Sabo says.

Feathers on birds also have different jobs: some provide insulation from the cold; others help birds fly; still others provide protection and make birds attractive to potential mates. By examining the color, size, shape, and texture of a feather, Sabo can tell which part of the bird it came from. Knowing where it came from on the bird helps her determine what purpose the feather served, and this, in turn, helps her identify the bird.

The wing feathers of an eagle and a turkey may seem similar at first glance, she says. But a closer look reveals that the eagle's wing feathers are very flat, helping the bird to soar, while the turkey's are curved, because it remains on the ground.

Clockwise from top: saw-whet owl; feathers from different bird species; peregrine falcon; forensic ornithologist examining bird bones; great gray owl in flight; wood duck

THE UNRAVELING

February 1994

While the Wildlife Detectives were examining evidence from the elk itself, the Wyoming State Crime Lab was studying the rifle that Porter had delivered to Agent Brown.

This Remington bolt-action rifle is similar to the one used to kill Charger. The scope is used for viewing and targeting animals.

Using a comparison microscope—two microscopes hooked together so that two objects can be viewed simultaneously—firearms expert Bob Christensen compares bullets and casings test-fired from the rifle with the bullets and casings found near Charger. He finds that the markings differ: this rifle "did not fire the shell casings recovered in Yellowstone National Park."

But if this was not the rifle that killed Charger, what rifle was used? Could it be another one that belonged to Porter? Forensic tests point in that direction. They reveal that some of the casings that the agents collected from Porter's apartment had been fired from the same rifle as the casings found near Charger.

Fortunately, at least one person knows the location of the real murder weapon. It is the mystery caller.

"I can't stand this," the caller tells Brown. "He's been bragging about how you guys would never catch him." The informant says that the poacher is hiding the rifle he had used until the situation cools down.

Brown immediately obtains a search warrant for the residence of Mr. Jack Porter.

March 8, 1994

From Pat Ozment's running log of the case: "Warrant was executed last night. Went well. Got .25-caliber rifle, casings and boxes of shells. Also seven spotlights, Franklin Planner, wife's journal and one video tape."

"When we seized the gun, he knew the gig was up," says Brown. Finding Mrs. Porter's journal also proved valuable, because she had kept a record of their activities.

The journal reveals that Porter was "a pretty regular poacher." "He did a lot of spotlighting," says Brown. That's when some poachers shine a spotlight on an animal so it will freeze and become an easy target.

The informant says that Charger died this way. Porter and an employee "drove around, saw the bull, and one of them—we don't know for sure who—decided he wanted it," says Brown.

Later that night Porter and his friend went back to Elk Park after dark, shone a spotlight on Charger, and shot him, Brown says. Soon after, "somebody came down the road with their headlights shining, so they jumped in the truck, took off, and came back an hour later. Then they ran out and cut off the skull cap and antlers, threw them in the back of the truck, covered

them up with a tarp, and drove straight through to Salt Lake City that night. They got home about two or three in the morning."

The story and the times agree with Mrs. Porter's journal—a journal she kept day to day, never suspecting that her husband's hunting habits were illegal.

September 1994

A federal grand jury in Cheyenne indicts Porter on three criminal counts. The first is a misdemeanor, charging him with killing the elk, removing its antlers, and transporting the rack across state lines from Wyoming to Utah in violation of the Lacey Act. Poaching in a national park is considered a misdemeanor instead of a felony if it is not done for commercial gain.

The second count charges him with felony witness tampering. After evidence was seized from his home, Porter tried to give a friend $5,000 to say that he had killed the elk.

The third count is a misdemeanor charging Porter with using his Sako brand .25-caliber rifle to kill the elk unlawfully.

Porter pleads guilty to all three charges.

Justice Is Served: April 3, 1995

Chief U.S. District Judge Alan B. Johnson accepts Porter's guilty plea, telling Porter that killing the elk was only "the first of several mistakes" he had made. The judge notes that "in October 1993, after the poaching of the Big Guy [Charger], Porter was arrested for taking elk and deer in a restricted area in Idaho." He also points to evidence showing that Porter illegally tracked animals using spotlights and purposely misled officials by giving them the wrong rifle.

"These are all things which you are going to have to search your soul about," he tells Porter. "You simply can't tap dance around or obstruct justice."*

Johnson sentences Porter to eight months in jail with half of that time to be served in his home, fines him $20,000, and orders him to pay $10,000 restitution to Yellowstone National Park. He also has to forfeit the rifle, valued at approximately $1,500, to park authorities. The judge places Porter on three years' supervised probation, which means that he cannot possess a firearm or hunt anywhere in the country during that time. In addition, Porter has to give up the antlers, which are estimated to be worth about $8,000 in the trophy market.

"This guy is like a lot of wildlife offenders," says Assistant U.S. Attorney Kip Crofts, who prosecuted the case. "For one reason or another they have a compulsion for big trophy animals, and the only ones left are in the national parks."

But that's not hunting, Crofts says. "It is like killing an animal in a zoo. These are not hunters. They are cowards and thieves—cowards who kill animals who've been taught to trust humans, and thieves who steal something irreplaceable from all of us."

Note the indentations on the bullet casings. Firearms experts compare these when looking for clues to solve wildlife crimes.

* *Denver Post,* April 3, 1995. Dates and circumstances are real.

Wild Work to Be Done

America's appetite for wildlife products seems to grow each year. Poachers know this—that's why they break wildlife laws and risk jail sentences—the profits from consumer sales are too big for some to ignore. Regrettably, about ninety percent of poachers get away with their crimes because of a shortage of money and manpower to stop them. The World Wildlife Fund reports that "up to one-quarter of all imported wildlife—both live animals and products—available in department stores, pet shops, and specialty catalogs may have entered the country illegally."

What can you do to help?

•Understand that laws alone will not stop poachers from illegally killing wildlife—poachers kill wild animals because people buy products made with them.

•Shop wisely: if you travel to another country, be sure to ask whether a wildlife product can be imported. For example, all sea turtle products are illegal to bring to the United States.

•Join with your family to support organizations, such as your local zoo, that work to save endangered species.

•Contact the U.S. Fish and Wildlife Service for information about a summer job at a wildlife refuge, research lab, or other areas open to young people through the Youth Conservation Corps.

Write to:
Director, U.S. Fish and Wildlife Service
Department of Interior
Washington, D.C. 20240

www.fws.gov

•Consider a career in wildlife forensics. The Forensic Sciences Foundation publishes a booklet that provides an excellent overview of forensic careers.

Write to:
The Forensic Sciences Foundation, Inc.
P.O. Box 669
Colorado Springs, CO 80901

Or contact the Wildlife Forensics Lab directly:
U.S. Fish and Wildlife Forensics Laboratory
1490 East Main Street
Ashland, OR 97520

Wildlife Forensic Terms

Caliber: The diameter of a bullet, which is one of the primary ways to identify a gun.

DNA (deoxyribonucleic acid): The chemical blueprint that makes people and animals what they are and provides genetic clues to identity.

Endangered species: Any species considered to be in immediate danger of extinction.

Firearms experts: Forensic specialists who examine and compare microscopic etchings on guns, bullets, cartridge cases, and so on, to help solve crimes.

Forensic ornithologist: A scientist who studies birds and identifies their remains to help solve wildlife crimes.

Morphologist: A forensic scientist who examines the form and structure of evidence such as furs, feathers, teeth, and claws to help identify animals and solve wildlife crimes.

National Eagle Repository: The U.S. government's collection and distribution center for bald eagles, golden eagles, and other raptors who have died from natural causes or the actions of people.

National Wildlife Property Repositor: A storehouse in Colorado containing wildlife parts and products that have been forfeited or abandoned to the U.S. Fish and Wildlife Service.

Necropsy: An examination of a dead animal to determine or confirm the cause of death.

Poacher: A person who hunts or fishes illegally.

Schreger lines: The tiny lines in ivory that can be seen under a microscope. Wildlife scientists use the differing patterns of these lines to distinguish between legal and illegal ivory.

Serologist: A scientist who analyzes blood and other body fluids to help solve crimes.

Threatened species: Any species that is likely to become endangered within the foreseeable future.

Tine: A branch of an elk's or deer's antlers.

Tool marks: The impressions left by weapons and other instruments used to commit a crime.

U.S. Fish and Wildlife Forensics Laboratory: The only forensics lab in the world dedicated to solving wildlife crimes, located in Ashland, Oregon.

Veterinary pathologist: A medical scientist who studies diseases and injuries of animals and uses this information to determine the cause and manner of an animal's death.

Wildlife special agents: The U.S. Fish and Wildlife Service professionals—there are about 200—who enforce laws related to the illegal taking and transporting of wildlife. Their jobs include everything from surveillance and undercover work to making arrests and testifying in court.

Wildlife inspectors: Experts in wildlife law and species identification who check for illegal animal parts and products at airports, shipping docks, and borders. The U.S. Fish and Wildlife Service employs about 85 inspectors nationwide.

Wildlife criminalist: Scientists who use scanning electron microscopes and other high-powered equipment to examine such things as powered rhino horn, ivory, and bear gallbladders.

Wildlife forensic science: The study and practice of applying science to solve wildlife crimes and settle legal matters. Its three goals are to identify the species in question; determine the cause of death; and connect the suspect to the crime.

Index

Page numbers in italics refer to photographs.